LET'S-READ-AND-FIND-OUT SCIENCE®

STAGE 2

Forces Make Things Move

By Kimberly Brubaker Bradley • Illustrated by Paul Meisel

HarperCollinsPublishers

The *Let's-Read-and-Find-Out Science* book series was originated by Dr. Franklyn M. Branley, Astronomer Emeritus and former Chairman of the American Museum–Hayden Planetarium, and was formerly co-edited by him and Dr. Roma Gans, Professor Emeritus of Childhood Education, Teachers College, Columbia University. Text and illustrations for each of the books in the series are checked for accuracy by an expert in the relevant field. For more information about Let's-Read-and-Find-Out Science books, write to HarperCollins Children's Books, 1350 Avenue of the Americas, New York, NY 10019, or visit our website at www.letsreadandfindout.com.

Library of Congress Cataloging-in-Publication Data
Bradley, Kimberly Brubaker.
  Forces make things move / by Kimberly Brubaker Bradley ; illustrated by Paul Meisel.— 1st ed.
    p. cm. — (Let's-read-and-find-out science. Stage 2)
Summary: Simple language and humorous illustrations show how forces make things move, prevent them from starting to move, and stop them from moving.
  ISBN 0-06-028906-6 — ISBN 0-06-028907-4 (lib. bdg.) — ISBN 0-06-445214-X (pbk.)
  1. Force and energy—Juvenile literature. 2. Friction—Juvenile literature.
3. Gravity—Juvenile literature. [1. Force and energy. 2. Friction. 3. Gravity.]
I. Meisel, Paul, ill. II. Title. III. Series.
QC73.4.B74 2005   2002014763
531'.6—dc21

Typography by Elynn Cohen   1 2 3 4 5 6 7 8 9 10   ❖   First Edition

To my family
—K.B.B.

If you push a toy car, you can make it move across the floor. Your push moves the car. Your push is a force.

Forces get things moving.

Forces also make things stop.

When the toy car rolls across the floor and stops, a force stopped it. Forces also make things speed up or slow down.

Any push or pull is a force. Forces can move things farther away or bring them closer. Some forces are very strong. Some are so weak, you can't feel them at all.

Nothing starts moving until it is pushed or pulled. If you don't push your toy car, it just sits there—unless something else pushes it, like the wind or your cat or your big brother. The wind, your cat, and your big brother can all produce force. The force moves your car. Any time your car is moving, a force made it start. The heavier an object is, the more force it takes to start it moving. If you want to run across the yard, your feet have to push on the ground to get you moving.

If you and your big brother decide to have a race, his feet will have to push harder on the ground than yours. Why? Because he weighs more. It takes more force to make him move.

Once you are running, only another force can stop you. Your feet push on the ground to make you stop. If you want to stop quickly, it takes more force than if you want to stop slowly. You'll have to push harder.

It takes a lot of force to start heavy things moving. That's why your living room couch doesn't fly across the room when you bump into it. It's why a breeze can't blow your family's car off the driveway. Other things, like leaves and papers and hats, don't weigh very much. Even tiny forces can make them fly around. A little wind makes enough force to make them move.

But if your big brother is lying on the living room couch, you're going to have to push pretty hard to force him off.

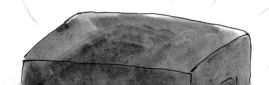

Whenever you push something, it pushes back against you.

If you push a toy car, it pushes back against you with the exact same force. If you push harder, the toy car pushes back harder! This can be difficult to understand, but it's true. The force you put on the car is always the same as the force the car puts on you.

If you push the toy car, your force makes the car start moving. So if the toy car is also pushing you, why don't you start moving? Because you are so much heavier than a toy car. Remember, it takes more force to move heavy things. The force that can move a toy car can't move you. Since it takes such a small amount of force to move the toy car, and the toy car puts only that much force on you, the force is too small for you to feel.

11

If you push your family's real car parked in your driveway, it pushes back too. Just like your toy car, the real car pushes back with the same amount of force as you put on it. If you push the real car gently, it pushes back gently. If you push harder, you can feel it push back harder.

12

You can't produce enough force to move the real car. Neither can your big brother.

Sometimes you can see what is pushing or pulling, and sometimes you can't. If you roll your toy car and it hits a wall or the couch, you can see that the wall or the couch stops the car. The wall and the couch produce force.

(If the car hits your big brother, you'd better run.)

15

If the car doesn't hit a wall or your big brother, or the couch or the cat or anything you can see, it still stops. What is pushing on the car to make it stop? A force called friction!

Everything is bumpy. Even things that feel smooth, like glass or ice, are still a little bit bumpy. You can't feel the bumps of glass— they are too small—and you can't see them either, but they are still there. Whenever two things rub against each other, the bumps on those things rub against each other. The force of the bumps rubbing against each other is called friction.

Friction makes moving things slow down. When you roll your car, the bumps on the floor push against the bumps on the car's wheels a little bit. This friction is the force that stops the car.

If you push the car along a shiny wooden hallway, it rolls much farther than if you push it along a thick bedroom rug. The rug is bumpier than the hallway. It creates more friction. It makes the car stop more quickly.

Wow. Look at mine go!!

Mine doesn't roll.

What if you roll your car across very slippery ice? It will go even farther than it does on the shiny wooden floor. The ice is so smooth that the force of friction is very small.

But even if the car isn't touching anything—even if you pretend it's an airplane and throw it right through the air—it still stops moving. It falls to the ground. Two forces stop it. One is friction. Even air has a small amount of friction.

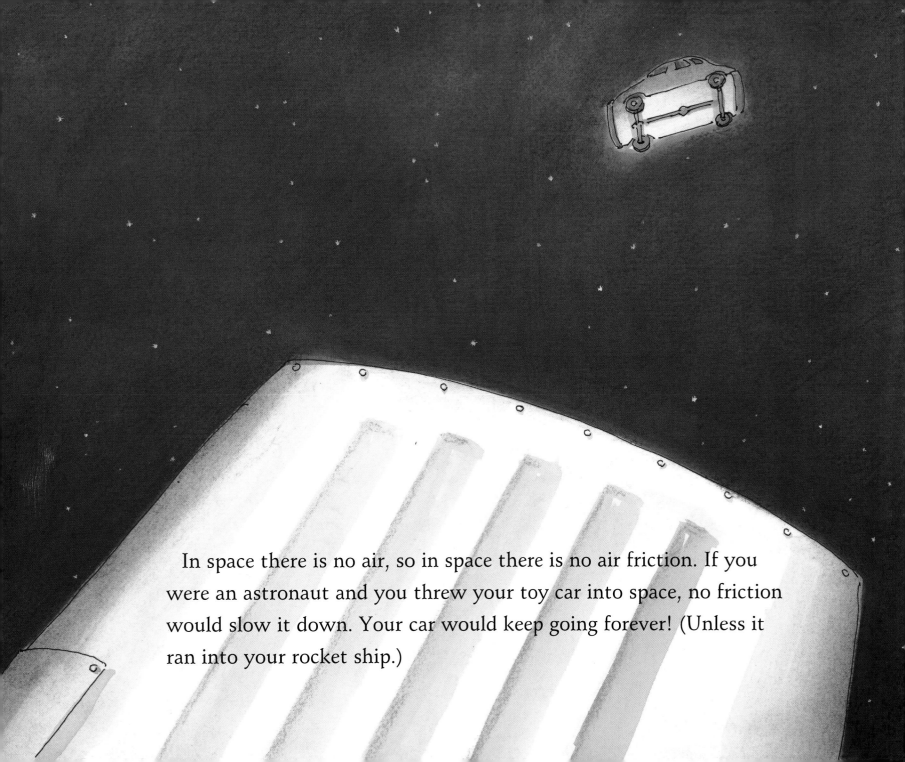

In space there is no air, so in space there is no air friction. If you were an astronaut and you threw your toy car into space, no friction would slow it down. Your car would keep going forever! (Unless it ran into your rocket ship.)

The second force that stops the car is called gravity. If you drop the car, it falls.

Why? Why doesn't it stay up? You haven't thrown it down. You haven't pushed it or pulled it. But it moved, so some other force must be pulling it down.

That force is called gravity. Gravity is the force that every object has for every other object.

Gravity at work!

You have gravity. Your big brother has gravity. If the two of you are standing on opposite sides of the room, you both have a tiny, tiny amount of gravity pulling you toward each other. You will never feel the force from this gravity. It is *much* too small.

23

The gravity force between any two objects depends on how much they weigh. Most of the time gravity is a teeny tiny force. When you hold a carrot in your hand, there is a gravity force between you and the carrot, but you'll never feel it. There is a gravity force between your big brother and your cat, but neither of them cares. You can feel the gravity between you and another object only if either you or that other object is really, really huge.

REALLY huge—like the size of the entire earth. The whole planet. Everyone can feel the earth's gravity! It's a big force. The earth's gravity pulls you, and everything else on or near the earth, down. It pulls things toward the center of the earth. If you dug a deep hole and dropped your big brother into it, he'd fall until he hit the bottom. The earth's gravity would pull him all the way down.

The earth has so much gravity that when we say gravity, we're almost always talking about the earth's gravity, not the gravity between you and your big brother or the gravity between a carrot and a cat.

Gravity is such a part of our everyday lives that you probably don't even think about it. If you spill a glass of milk, you expect it to spill down, onto the floor, rather than up, onto the ceiling. If you let go of your toy car, you expect it to fall to the ground. If you throw your car across the room, you expect it to end up on the floor, not suspended halfway up the living room wall.

Gravity is why apples on trees fall down to the ground, instead of staying up in the sky. Gravity makes it hard to throw a baseball all the way to the moon. It's why your parents' cars stay on the ground instead of soaring through the air. It's why rockets to space have such huge engines—the big engines make enough force to be stronger than gravity.

Forces are all around us. Forces make things go faster and slower. They make things stop. They make things start. Forces get things moving.

FIND OUT MORE ABOUT FRICTION

You will need:

2 toy cars, the same size
2 boards, the same size
2 chairs, the same size

a long, empty space on the floor
sandpaper, towels, waxed paper, foil, felt,
and other things with rough or smooth
surfaces

Put one end of each board on the seat of a chair and the other end on the floor. Set up both chairs so that you can run the toy cars down the boards and across the open space on the floor. Make sure both boards are raised to the same height. When you set the toy cars on the top ends of the boards and let go, the cars should travel about the same distance across the floor.

Now put a piece of sandpaper on the floor against the end of one of the boards. Run both cars down the boards again. Which one went farthest? Can you guess why?

Now replace the sandpaper with a towel. Which car travels farther now? Does the car that had to go across the towel travel farther than the one that went across sandpaper? Can you guess why or why not? Which produces more friction, the sandpaper or the towel?

Run the cars over different surfaces. Each surface—sandpaper, towel, waxed paper—will create a different amount of friction. The surface that makes the most friction will slow the car the most, and that car will travel the shortest distance.

When you run the cars down the boards instead of pushing them with your hands, you are letting gravity pull the cars. The force of gravity will always be the same, but the force you would use to push might not be. It would be very hard for you to tell if you were pushing the cars with the same force each time. In this test you want to pay attention to the forces of friction, so it's best to let gravity move the cars.